HOW TO STUFF DONE WHEN YOU HAVE ADHD

The Power of Pomodoro Technique

Mitchell White

Copyright © 2020

TABLE OF CONTENTS

INTRODUCTION

In the simplest of terms, ADHD, Attention-deficit/hyperactivity disorder, is a common condition caused by differences in the brain. This justifies why persons with ADHD find it quite challenging to focus, while some are usually impulsive and hyperactive. ADHD isn't age-oriented; it happens to both kids and adult.

Should you find it hard to keep still, to focus, and sometimes think things through before acting them out, then you may begin to consider yourself having ADHD. This condition may also influence how individuals manage their emotion – basically, this set of person battle with managing their emotions, and also other intra-personal skills. Albeit, the main trouble common to everyone with ADHD is focusing.

As mentioned above, persons with ADHD also encounter issues when managing a few key skills, which may be referred to as "executive functions." And, of course, this established certain degrees of challenges, which cuts across several areas, in their lives, ranging from work to school, to everyday living, and so on. Apart from finding it hard to manage their emotions, you may also struggle to follow directions, instructions, and ultimately fail at being organized.

You should, however, know that ADHD isn't synonymous to being lazy or lacking inertia (read as willpower), as many see it to be. More often than not, you will find individuals with Attention-deficit/hyperactivity disorder trying even harder than others to find focus and keep their impulses on the check. But then, unfortunately, a few of them fail or simply continue to struggle.

Long before now, people are used to tagging ADHD for kids alone, especially boys. However, over time research and personal experiences have proven this notion wrong as it shows that adults also struggle with ADHD, even to apparent degrees. Also, we may be safe to say that the feminine gender experience ADHD up to the extent at which men and boys do too. So, there really aren't any imbalances in this regard as both genders have almost the same share of the piece of cake.

Attention-deficit/hyperactivity disorder is accompanied by a number of symptoms, including inattention – i.e., being unable to keep focus, excessive movements, which often doesn't fit into the setting – say hyperactivity, performing actions that haven't been thought about at all – impulsiveness. However, you must know that individuals with ADHD do not always have a fair and equal share of these symptoms. This translates that people may experience these symptoms, and even more, at varying extents. And, of course, not everyone with Attention-deficit/hyperactivity disorder has all three symptoms as described above. Also, these symptoms may begin to vary, while some entirely wane as one move progressively in age.

In a nutshell, hyperactivity, impulsiveness, and inability to keep focus causes individuals of this kind to have real troubles with the management system of their brains. In this regard, persons suffering from Attention-deficit/hyperactivity disorder, more often than not, will find themselves struggling with managing their time, setting their priorities right, being able to get and stay organized, making plans aforetime of execution, managing their emotions, being able to pay attention, they may also struggle to remember things, constant shifting of focus from one thing to another, which causes them to have loads of unfinished tasks on their desks, and so on. Really, there are several consequences in this regard.

But for them, of all these symptoms and signs that accompany Attention-deficit/hyperactivity disorder, hyper-focusing is one of such that people find quite confusing. It should no longer be news that persons with ADHD find it hard to stay on a job. However, once they find any activity or task interesting, they begin to show signs of "forever" therein. That is, they hyper-focus on such tasks, and consequently waste valuable time unnecessarily. For example, you may find an adult getting so engrossed in a TV show or video game, to the point that they do not know they're being called. Sometimes it's drifting from planning to cook to being buried in the middle of a magazine that caught your interest – basically, there are several instances in this regard.

Consequently, there have been several types of research within the past years, all in the bid of getting the exact possible causes of ADHD. And this may be touted as what led to discoveries that established both the similarities and differences in people with and without attention-deficit/hyperactivity disorder. Overall, these researches agree that the way the brain develops in each situation is similar, just that the areas involved in executive function take longer to develop in people with ADHD. And this may be linked to why individuals with ADHD may act lesser than their age – say three years younger. However, it is imperative to note that this striking difference has absolutely nothing to do with intelligence. In essence, individuals with Attention-deficit/hyperactivity disorder as just as smarts as their counterparts who do not have it.

For children, their teachers, school staff, guardian, or even their parents may provide doctors with the right and adequate information to help them evaluate the learning and behavioral problems of such a child; consequently, proffer assistance with behavioral training. Nonetheless, under no circumstance should teachers or school staff diagnose or administer treatments or solutions of any kind to kids with Attention-deficit/hyperactivity disorder, as they aren't in the right position to do such. Only parent, under the supervision of their physician, in most cases, can do such.

However, for adults, a better percentage of them do not know that they have this disorder, and, therefore, do not address it as quickly as possible. More often than not, even, these categories of adults already have ADHD since when they were a child – but still, they do not know.

In this regard, anyways, a comprehensive evaluation and analysis, which typically includes the review of both current and past symptoms, a medical exam and history, and use of a few more adult checklists. Basically, adults with Attention-deficit/hyperactivity disorder may be treated with psychotherapy, medication, or both, as the case may be. More often too, such adults may engage in some behavioral management strategies, which includes ways to reduce distractions and at the same time, increase organization and structure.

Again, ADHD isn't a kind of disorder that just goes away as people grow in age, most especially troubles to keep focus. Unless something is done, adults may experience Attention-deficit/hyperactivity disorder until death.

Now, irrespective of when you get diagnosed with Attention-deficit/hyperactivity disorder – it maybe since you were a child or now that you've become a grown-up, there are still certain treatments and strategies that you can undergo or execute, which effectively manages the symptoms. And also, there are certain supports that can make things easier for you both at work, home, social gatherings, and other places that you may function at.

The thing is there is basically nothing to fret about being diagnosed with ADHD. From my experience, I have met several persons with Attention-deficit/hyperactivity disorder who live both a full and happy life. In this regard, I must say that treatment helps a great deal, and of course, it is quite essential that you pay unwavering attention to the signs and symptoms that it gives, plus visit your doctor regular too.

However, there are cases whereby treatments and medications that were once effective cease to work. Sometimes you may need to change such treatment plan – it may be as a result of your body system overgrowing such treatment plan. Albeit, as much as it is inarguable that your body may outgrow certain treatments and medications, it is imperative that you are aware of certain strategies that have proven over time to be the best solution approach to Attention-deficit/hyperactivity disorder, especially as an adult. The Pomodoro Technique. In subsequent chapters, I will be delving dee right into everything that you should know about the Pomodoro Technique, and how it concerns adults with Attention-deficit/hyperactivity disorder.

In this guide, I have comprehensively, from experience and my wealth of knowledge explained the right and proper ways individuals diagnosed with Attention-deficit/hyperactivity disorder can get things done via the use of the Pomodoro Technique. Here, you will get to know what exactly your ADHD problems are, and in tandem, how to get such issues solves via the use of the Pomodoro Technique.

This promises to be an interesting and exciting and informative ride; I really can't wait to begin any longer!

Chapter One
How to know if you have
ADHD

Attention-deficit/hyperactivity disorder, as mentioned is a neurological condition marked by symptoms of inattention and/or hyperactive impulsivity, which in turn, interferes with daily functioning in at least two settings — for instance, at work and home. In this regard, most adults who's got symptoms of ADHD are most likely to have experienced such when they were much younger too. However, now, how such symptoms manifest in adults may tend to change of shift as they continue to age. And again, rather also unfortunate, a better percentage of adults who experience Attention-deficit/hyperactivity disorder have never been diagnosed.

Untreated or unattended to Attention-deficit/hyperactivity disorder can result to several physical and mental problems, which doesn't only establish a considerable level of strain on relationships that these set of people are, but also causes an extensive range of difficulties cut across several aspects of their everyday living. As much as the Pomodoro Technique may be a very efficient tool to addressing ADHD, it is quite vital that you recognize these signs of ADHD, especially as an adult, so you can begin to address it as soon as possible.

In this chapter, I have curated a comprehensive outline of ADHD symptoms both in adults and children, too, while paying a greater extent of focus on adults. Keep reading to learn more about the symptoms of Attention-deficit/hyperactivity disorder.

Signs and Symptoms of ADHD In Children

Diagnosis of ADHD in children usually happens before such a child turns seven. Overall, ADHD in children is quite challenging to identify, as more often than not, their symptoms may be mistaken to be the normal kid behaviour. For example, we all know kids who will never sit still, who will never listen, who detests the following instruction no matter how clearly such an instruction may seem. Also, you may find this set of kids blurting our inappropriate comment, and often at inappropriate times too. Sometimes, we label these kids as troublemakers or being undisciplined and lazy, when in the real sense, they are actually having a fair share of Attention-deficit/hyperactivity disorder.

However, despite how hard it may seem to distinguish between ADHD and regular kid behaviour, a few distinguishing symptoms may help in this regard. When you discover one or more of these symptoms across all situations and settings, then such a child may have ADHD – now is the time to take a closer look at such a child.

Overall, children with ADHD may be:

- Inattentive, but not hyperactive or impulsive.
- Hyperactive and impulsive, but able to pay attention.
- Inattentive, hyperactive, and impulsive (the most common form of ADHD).

So, briefly, I would be explaining each bullet points of symptoms in children, after which we keep it locked there for children, and concentrate exclusively on adults.

Inattentiveness signs and symptoms of ADHD

Now, don't get this wrong; it isn't as if children with Attention-deficit/hyperactivity disorder cannot pay attention. Not, not in that manner. Factually, when such a child is doing things that he or she enjoys or has interests in, you can trust them not to have any iota of trouble being focused, attentive, and staying on the task or topic. However, over time, the task may become repetitive and thus boring, which may cause them to tune out completely.

Staying on track is yet another common problem amongst children with ADHD. That is, you fill usually find them bouncing from one task to another, yet without completing any of them – not even to an appreciable extent. You may also find them skipping some steps and procedures when executing tasks. Organizing their schoolwork is also a hard feat for them to overcome – usually harder than for other children; it's very noticeable. For them to stay focused, then need a very calm and quiet environment.

Symptoms of inattention in children with ADHD include:

They have trouble keeping their focus on singular tasks. That is, they are easily distracted, and quickly get bored with tasks, even before such a task gets completed.

> ➢ Doesn't give listening ears.
> ➢ Such children also experience difficulties when remembering things. Remember that they do not give listening ears; neither do they pay attention. Therefore, they tend to forget things very quickly.
> ➢ Have issues planning ahead of situations, staying organized, and finishing projects.

Hyperactivity signs and symptoms of ADHD

Another conspicuous sign of Attention-deficit/hyperactivity disorder in children is hyperactivity. Inarguably, it is quite typical for kids to be active. However, for those with hyperactive symptoms of

Attention-deficit/hyperactivity disorder, they are always on the move. You will always find them trying to do several things all at the same time – they literally bounce from one task to another. And even when you force them to stay still, the high degree of difficulty that they go through doesn't take too long to show on their faces, and also in their body actions too; you may either find them tapping their feet, playing with their fingers, or shaking their legs.

Symptoms of hyperactivity in children ADHD include:

> Constantly squirms and fidgets.
> Finds it really hard to sit still, quiet, or relaxed. They tend to always be all over the place.
> This makes them move around always, sometimes without a specific aim – they just need to move.
> They talk too much – this isn't too much of a yardstick, anyways.
> They are quite temperamental.

Impulsive signs and symptoms of ADHD

Finally, children with Attention-deficit/hyperactivity disorder experience real issues with controlling themselves – they are usually spontaneous. They do not know how to censor themselves as other children do. You will find them interrupting conversations, invading others' spaces, asking questions with relevance in class, make tactless observations, and so on. Overall, they also do not know how to control themselves to stay still and patient.

Their impulsiveness may also cause them to be weird, moody, overreact to things, needy, and perhaps clingy.

Overall, symptoms of impulsivity in children ADHD include:

> They do things without proper thought.
> You will catch them guessing in the situation instead of taking time to tackle such a question. But then, they may be good guessers too.

➤ Children with ADHD are intruders too. You will often find them interrupting others' games, conversations, and all.

➤ They find it difficult to censor their emotions. Their impulsiveness may cause them to be temperamental.

Signs and Symptoms of ADHD In Adults

As an adult, it is quite advisable that you strike a balance in life. However, should you find yourself always being late, forgetful, disorganized, or overwhelmed by your responsibilities in almost all the settings that you find yourself in, then you may have attention-deficit/hyperactivity disorder. ADHD affects several adults and shows an extensive range of symptoms, frustrating enough that they may cost such an adult many things, including career, relationships, opportunities, and so on.

Although scientists aren't so sure of what the causes of ADHD are, it is quite notable, well from my experience and knowledge, that there is a substantial likelihood that Attention-deficit/hyperactivity disorder is caused by a combination of environment, genes, and differences in how the brain is wired. And also, being diagnosed with ADHD may tell that you have actually carried a few of the symptoms you are experiencing from childhood into adulthood. Why? Well, more often than not Attention-deficit/hyperactivity disorder goes unrecognized throughout childhood, especially in the past, when only a few persons were aware of the disorder. Children are often labelled as dreamers, goof-offs, slackers, troublemakers, and all sorts, by their teachers, guardian, or even their family, when in the real sense, they only have ADHD. Also, you may have been able to contain the symptoms of ADHD. At the same time, you were younger, however, as you age on, you run into more responsibilities and tasks, including pursuing a career, running a household, raising a family, and so on, which is actually normal.

Consequently, you may begin to fail in containing these symptoms, which in no time may become quite evident. The thing is the more your responsibilities, the more the demand on your abilities to remain focused, organized, and calm. And, really, this can turn out to be challenging for everybody.

However, the good thing about Attention-deficit/hyperactivity disorder is that no matter how overwhelming it feels, the challenges of ADHD are beatable. With the right extents of education, support, and strategy, you can learn how to manage the symptoms of ADHD as an adult adequately. And you may even find yourself ultimately turning these weaknesses into strengths. As an adult, it is never too hard to turn your difficulties with ADHD around and make it a success for you. Really, it is possible.

ADHD is more often than not different in adults than it does in children – I mean the symptoms. And, interestingly, these symptoms are quite unique for each person. This translates that these symptoms are quite vast. Nonetheless, in this section, I have categorized these symptoms of adult Attention-deficit/hyperactivity disorder into five. Do your best in identifying the areas where you experience difficulty. Once you discover your most problematic symptoms, you can start implementing strategies for dealing with them – most notably, Pomodoro Technique (I have discussed this extensively in chapter 5 of this book).

Trouble concentrating and staying focused

In simple term, this means "Attention deficit." However, this term may be misleading, as in the real sense adults with Attention-deficit/hyperactivity disorder are actually capable of staying focus on tasks and activities, although, they need to find such a task engaging or stimulating or interesting firstly; this isn't restricted to specific tasks too. Notwithstanding, in the same vein, these same persons get easily distracted by irrelevant sounds and sights, and consequently hop from one task to another task. Adults with ADHD also get bored very quickly.

However, you will often find yourself disregarding or overlooking symptoms in this category because they are mostly less outwardly disruptive, especially when compared to other categories of symptoms such as impulsivity and hyperactivity. Although, they can be a bit as troublesome as these other symptoms too.

The symptoms in this category include:

- Adults with ADHD are easily distracted, especially by irrelevant and low-priority activities and events that they're supposed to ignore under normal circumstances.

- They are usually jampacked with several conflicting thoughts, such that they find it really hard to choose and follow one, even if it's the wrong one.

- They may find it hard to pay rapt attention or to focus – for example, when reading or listening. This also pertains to being easily distracted. And this accounts for why they find it hard to keep up with conversations too.

- Adults with Attention-deficit/hyperactivity disorder may get zoned out too often and very quick, even without realizing that they are zoning out.

One of their greatest nightmares is finishing tasks, no matter how easy such a task may be – they don't just know how to do it. This justifies why you usually find yourself having several jobs and tasks on your desk, waiting to be completed.

- They have difficulty in remembering things, such as directions, instructions, and so on.

- Adults with ADHD gets bored easily and quickly too. This happens especially when what such an adult is doing goes in a circle – that is, if it is a repetitive task.

Disorganization and forgetfulness

Another symptom is being disorganized and forgetful. Whether consciously or unconsciously, adults suffering from Attention-deficit/hyperactivity disorder often find life in chaos and out of control. And in this regard, staying organized may top the list of things that they find challenging. By being organized, I mean sorting out what information is relevant for the task at hand, keeping track of tasks and responsibilities, prioritizing your to-do list, and managing your time.

Overall, general symptoms of disorganization and forgetfulness in adults ADHD include:

- Adults with Attention-deficit/hyperactivity disorder may be very poor at organizational skills, either at home, office, car or even on their desk. You will always find their immediate environment messy, stuffy, and clustered, except, of course, they employ someone to do justice to that for them.

- They are excellent procrastinators. They procrastinate almost everything that they want to do.

- They are experiencing challenges starting a project. But then, finishing such a project is yet another challenge.

- Adults with ADHD also experience chronic lateness. And this is caused by their quick and intense level of forgetfulness. They forget almost everything, including deadlines, commitments, and appointments.

- They are careless. You will find yourself losing items too often.

- Underestimating the time that it will take them to complete tasks.

Impulsivity

Suffering from symptoms in this category translates that you may experience issues inhibiting your comments, behaviours, and responses. More often than not, you will find yourself acting before putting it to proper consideration, or reacting without considering the consequences. You may also find yourself interrupting others, giving comments without thinking it through, and even rushing to execute tasks without considering to read the attached instructions.

Overall, symptoms of impulsivity include finding it extremely hard to remain patient and calm. For better or for worse, you may dive headlong into situations and find yourself in potentially risky circumstances.

General symptoms categorized under impulsivity are:

- More often than not, you will find yourself interrupting others when talking. This, however, happens by reflex, and usually, you won't be able to control it. It doesn't mean you aren't intelligent or not courteous enough. It's just your nature.

- Experience challenges or difficulties in controlling oneself. Adults with ADHD exhibit more addictive tendencies than others who aren't.

- They often blurt out rude or inappropriate comments. And this is as a result of not thinking their words through before saying them out.

- They are reckless and spontaneous actors with utmost disregard for the ensuing consequences.

- They experience trouble behaving in ways that are appropriate socially. For instance, they find it hard to sit long hours in a meeting.

Emotional difficulties

Another not-too-conspicuous category of symptoms in several adults with Attention-deficit/hyperactivity disorder is difficulty in managing their feelings, most notably, frustration, anger, and other related emotions. We may, therefore, infer that they may be temperamental.

Emotional symptoms of an adult with Attention-deficit/hyperactivity disorder include:

- You may easily get stressed out or flustered.
- Often, you will get irritated, and consequently, explode in hot temper – sometimes too much that what you yourself can contain.
- You may also suffer low self-esteem. There's also the problem of underachievement and insecurity.

- As an adult with ADHD, you may also find it hard staying motivated.

- You may also exhibit an intense sensitiveness to criticism, and may find yourself hiding from critics.

Hyperactivity or restlessness

Lastly, you may experience restlessness and hyperactivity as an adult with ADHD. You may be excessively energetic, and perpetually always on-the-move, as if on autopilot. However, we do not and can't always make use of this symptom as a yardstick to determine if you have ADHD or the extent at which you have the disorder. This is basically because of its relationship with age – as you grow older, the lesser you begin to get less restless and hyperactive as they now gradually go internal and subtle.

Nonetheless, general symptoms of hyperactivity and restlessness in adults with Attention-deficit/hyperactivity disorder include:

- An intense feeling of inner agitation, anxiety, racing thoughts, and so on may overwhelm you quite often – more than usual.

- You will always crave excitement, and consequently take risks even without putting them to proper considerations and thoughts. Boredom is also constant.

- You will always have the thoughts that you have some kind of superpowers that can make you do a million things all at once.

- You can't sit still for too long too. You will almost always find yourself shaking at least a part of your body, or better yet change your entire position.

- Adults with ADHD may portray signs of restlessness to by talking just too much – they are born talkative.

However, you should know that you do not have to be hyperactive to have ADHD. Basically, as mentioned afore-now, as you age, the likelihood of hyperactivity and restlessness tends to reduce. And at the moment, only a small percentage of adults with Attention-deficit/hyperactivity disorder suffer from this particular symptom.

Also, to be confident and utmost sure that you have adult Attention-deficit/hyperactivity disorder, you may also take the below interactive Attention-deficit/hyperactivity disorder symptom test. All you need to do is to provide a sincere yes or no answer to each question below.

1. I have difficulty getting organized.
2. When given a task, I am used to procrastinating instead of doing it immediately.

3. I work on a lot of projects all at a time, but can't seem to finish most of these projects.

4. I tend to make decisions and act on them impulsively, without thinking such decisions through. This includes getting sexually involved with someone spending money, diving into new activities, changing plans, and so on.

5. I get bored easily.

6. No matter how much I do or how hard I try, I just can't seem to reach my goals.

7. I often get distracted when people are talking; I just tune out or drift off.

8. I get so wrapped up in some things I do that I can hardly stop to take a break or switch to doing something else.

9. I tend to overdo things even when they're not good for me — like compulsive shopping, drinking too much, overworking, and overeating.

10. I get frustrated easily, and I get impatient when things are going too slowly.

11. My self-esteem is not as high as that of others I know.

12. I need a lot of stimulation from things like action movies and video games, new purchases, being among lively friends, driving fast or engaging in extreme sports.

13. I tend to say or do things without thinking, and sometimes that gets me into trouble.

14. I'd instead do things my way than follow the rules and procedures of others.

15. I often find myself tapping a pencil, swinging my leg, or doing something else to work off nervous energy.

16. I can feel suddenly down when I'm separated from people, projects or things that I like to be involved with.

17. I see myself differently than others see me, and when someone gets angry with me for doing something that upset them, I'm often very surprised.

18. Even though I worry a lot about dangerous things that are unlikely to happen to me, I tend to be careless and accident-prone.

19. Even though I have a lot of fears, people would describe me as a risk-taker.

20. I make a lot of careless mistakes.

21. I have blood relatives who suffer from ADHD, another neurological disorder, or substance abuse.

If you answered in the affirmative – yes, to at least fifteen of these questions, you show strong signs of attention deficit hyperactivity disorder (ADHD), and now is the time to take action.

People With ADHD Have Different Brains

From experience, I would be safe to say that Attention-deficit/hyperactivity disorder is more of a neurological disorder more than a behavioral one. Well, my claims have been backed up by a few scientists too – so, most likely, I am right. Asides that, we can evidently see that the brain structures of persons with Attention-deficit/hyperactivity disorder are slightly but significantly different from those of individuals who are growing normally. By normally, I mean persons who do not have the disorder.

Also, a few brain scans of a few of my past clients revealed that individuals with Attention-deficit/hyperactivity disorder have smaller five brain regions, which includes the amygdala, the hippocampus, the caudate nucleus, the nucleus accumbent, and the putamen. The amygdala is an almond-shaped structure which is involved in the processing of human emotions, including pleasure and fear. The hippocampus similarly holds significance in the memory, emotion, and learning of an individual. Finally, caudate nucleus, the nucleus accumbent, and the putamen are all brain structures within the striatum, and are responsible for the processing of dopamine, helping to control pleasure and motivation, and actively involved in the reward system of the brain.

Bearing in mind that these brain differences between persons with ADHD and those without are relatively small, you should also know that these differences get more dramatic with age. And this justifies my earlier claim that Attention-deficit/hyperactivity disorder may be caused by delayed development of the brain. The scenario is always as if the brains of those with ADHD are running – developing and maturing – to catch up with those who do not have the disorder.

Also, it is noteworthy to mention that the more the severity of these ADHD symptoms in an adult, the more the brain differences. This accounts why some areas of the brain, for example, those involved in inhibition, impulse control, concentration, and motor activity, are quite smaller.

Also, the white and grey matter in adults with ADHD are usually different from those who do not have the same disorder. In this regard, individuals with Attention-deficit/hyperactivity disorder may have a distinct neural pathway in areas of their brain that is involved in inhibition, impulse control, concentration, and motor activity. And these different pathways partly justify why individuals with ADHD often experience learning difficulties and behavioral issues.

Time Zones in ADHD – Now / Not Now

Two time zones exist for persons with the Attention-deficit/hyperactivity disorder, namely the "now and not now" time zones. These time zones can be easily understood as they are quite logical – let me break it down for you:

If the event isn't happening now, adults with ADHD tend to procrastinate until such an event, it quite close to the "now" time zone. This justifies why kids are usually told that everything is now. But then, that can work for adults, except we merely want to dwell in the world of fallacy and deceit. I mean, as an adult you understand things better and more clearly – you can't be easily deceived or cajoled into doing or believing something. Besides, as adults, it isn't always clear to know when to switch ourselves from the "not now" zone to the "now" zone.

So, instead of the typical procedure of having an internal clock which notifies when time is passing or being wasted, persons with ADHD experience their time from these two kinds of time zones. So, basically, what these zones mean is; if it isn't happening now, then it is happening not now. And if it is happening now, then it can't wait till later then, which means that things that are under the not now time zone do not need to be attended to at the moment.

And this also justifies why a better percentage of adults with Attention-deficit/hyperactivity disorder perform better when subjected to pressure. However, to adults who do not have the Attention-deficit/hyperactivity disorder, this time zones may appear maddening or as a mystery. Ultimately, it may also have a negative impact on several areas of such adults' life, including family, relationships, people's perception of them, career, and so on.

The now and not now time zones are excellent sources of regulators for persons that suffer from the ADHD disorder. They serve as alarms and timers. Basically, we would be safe to refer to these time zones as your internal memory or clock.

CHAPTER TWO

ADHD 'N'

PROCRASTINATION

Literally, everybody procrastinates. Although there are varying levels to it. When given a task that we do not just want to do, or have the right motivation to do, a better percentage of us will put such work off till the next day. While some may set the task aside till they get a clearer head, or when they feel less overwhelmed with other pressing responsibilities too. Some may just await a new day to start the job, alongside fresh energy.

However, as procrastination begins to seep into one's activities and gradually become a habit, problems may start to occur. And as I have said earlier, there are levels to this thing called procrastination.

Now, there is chronic procrastination. This kind of procrastination is what adults with Attention-deficit/hyperactivity disorder (ADHD) struggle with. And, of course, this kind of procrastination may cause unamendable problems at work, especially when job responsibilities aren't carried out as and when due but the last minute. It may ultimately cause such a person to lose his or her job.

Chronic procrastination that adults with ADHD struggle with may also result in financial stress at home, when you continually delay balancing the chequebook, or when you fail to pay your bills as quickly as possible. It may also lead to issues in your relationship, as you will appear too nonchalant or as a snub who performs excellently well in putting others off or making them feel less important.

Basically, there are several factors concerned in this regard. Albeit, here are some of the factors that can be at play in the relationship between ADHD and procrastination.

1. Problems Getting Started

For adults with the Attention-deficit/hyperactivity disorder, they may find it very hard and challenging to get started on a task, especially if such a task is one that is not intrinsically interesting. When one is, to an appreciable extent, distracted by outside elements, alongside internal thoughts too, such a person may find it hard even to locate the starting line, talk less of commencing such a task.

Often, the challenge that adults with ADHD face are figuring how and where exactly to start. Organizational problems may also come into play as you will find yourself continually struggling to plan, prioritize, and sequence tasks that you need to do before you can actually get started and also stay on track.

2. Getting Sidetracked

Once you eventually get started, you may as well discover that you easily and quickly become sidetracked by something else that is more exciting. This way, you further delay the original task. In other words, your attention as an adult with the Attention-deficit/hyperactivity disorder isn't stable, and regulating it may be complicated.

Of course, you can eventually get your attention exclusively focused on a task. However, despite this, you may also find it difficult to sustain such attention on the task, as you will catch our mind wandering almost always. This translates that you may find it hard to stay motivated, alert, and also on track, especially when you are not too interested or excited by the task at hand.

Also, you will discover that you delay tasks that are particularly boring or tedious to you up till the very last minute. At this point, your motivation to finally get started and ultimately complete the project is most likely drawn from the pressure of the approaching deadline. The worst-case scenario that may also happen in this regard is to get stuck not completing the task, thereby have to face all the ensuing consequences.

3. Last-Minute Propulsion

Another rather interesting thing about persons with Attention-deficit/hyperactivity disorder is outing off tasks until the very last minutes, which can ultimately establish an emergency-type situation, which may, in turn, propel this category of persons forward to get the job done successfully. This explains why some adults get extremely focused on completing tasks when deadlines are fast-approaching, and sometimes also, the immediacy of the negative consequences that will follow if the deadline isn't met.

However, this isn't advisable nor hygienic. Reason being that this urgency may create some levels of anxiety and stress, which consequently can affect both you and those around you, tremendously. Also, jobs that are completed in a rush tend not to be as standardized and qualitative as they should have been if such an adult hasn't procrastinated.

4. A Sense of Paralysis and Feeling Overwhelmed

Adults that suffer from Attention-deficit/hyperactivity disorder may occasionally experience a painful feeling of paralysis when they are to handle a project, especially during the starting stage. In essence, adults with ADHD may experience a sharp and painful sense of wanting to start a project, yet being unable to make considerable progress irrespective of the manner of such progress.

This may result in intense pressure too. The pressure that comes with knowing that you need to get started on a task, yet finding it hard to get moving.

5. Impaired Sense of Time

Sometimes, an impaired sense of time may lead to problems with getting started on a job. This translates that if you are having issues with estimating the time that one will take to complete a task, there is a higher likelihood of putting such a task off. The ideology in play here is that when you do not know or have a near-accurate estimation of how long it will take to complete a task, your subconscious may make you believe that you still have so much more time till such tasks are completed.

Also, Attention-deficit/hyperactivity disorder might cause sufferers to experience difficulty in tracking the passage of time. Failure to correctly track the passage of time may result in a case whereby deadlines sneak up even before one reckons with what is happening.

6. Fear of Failure

There can be a number of ADHD-related factors that lead to chronic procrastination, including distractibility, forgetfulness, disorganization, problems with prioritizing, sequencing, and time management.

In addition, if you have experienced repeated frustrations on certain types of tasks, you may naturally avoid those tasks to prevent the negative feelings that working on those tasks can bring about.

Sometimes there can be so much anxiety associated with starting the task that those feelings create an even more significant obstacle. The fear of not doing the task correctly, fear of imperfection, and fear of failure can all add to the procrastination.

CHAPTER THREE

ADHD SOLUTIONS – HOW

TO GET STUFF DONE WHEN

YOU HAVE ADHD

Every day, as humans, we are always faced with several – perhaps unlimited – interruptions, information, distractions and disruptions, work, and some other stuff. All these elements sum up against just one thing that remains finite, which is time. Consequently, getting things done, on time, efficiently, and effectively, becomes problematic.

And then, there's the internet – the present generation wizard. Inarguably, spending time on the web is an extreme source of temptation for everybody, especially if you are an adult with Attention-deficit/hyperactivity disorder. As much as the internet is also an excellent source of information, in unrestricted volumes, for problem-solving reasons, satisfying curiosity, and researching on a topic, it also offers a fair share of distraction to its users as it more often than not gets in the way of getting things done, not only effectively but also timely. Persons with the Attention-deficit/hyperactivity disorder usually find themselves caught in the web of being lost when hunting information and the excitement of discovering new things and ideas on the web. In this regard, we must apply the brakes on our searches.

For instance, an individual with Attention-deficit/hyperactivity disorder may catch herself spending more than usual time on researching how to get ink stains off her child's jeans. Over time, she learned to caution herself from going too deep and wide when sourcing for information. Consequently, in this regard, you will find such adults spending incredibly lesser time on low-consequence items and issues such as that, and instead, concentrate more on finding items like ADHD-friendly foods that have high protein content.

Persons with Attention-deficit/hyperactivity disorder confronts several challenges daily, weekly, and even all-round the year. Tandem to this realization, in this chapter, you will be learning a few useful strategies other than the Pomodoro Technique on how to get things done, especially as an individual with ADHD. In the next chapter, after this, I have compiled a comprehensive note on everything you need to know about the Pomodoro Technique too.

As someone with ADHD, you will always get confronted with special challenges in remaining productive or bettering your level of productivity. I mean, not even at the moment where there are several easily accessible distractions such as the internet, TV, email, social media, and so on. So, solving ADHD boils down to narrowing your options of distractions – i.e., managing distractions.

Below are my trusted schemes (read as strategies) of managing distractions and ultimately boosting your level of productivity, despite that you struggle with the Attention-deficit/hyperactivity disorder.

Get specific

In other to get things done timely and well when you struggle with ADHD, it is essential that you know what exactly needs to be done, and what doesn't need to be done. And this is where the different time zones explained in the introductory chapters come into play. The thing is, if you aren't specific and intentional about the things you want and need to do, you may just see yourself whiling away with time – not that you won't be busy, in fact, often you will be busy throughout the day, just that you may not be doing the right things. You may just be busy doing the "not now" things when the "now" things are left pending.

However, you may be overwhelmed with internal resistance or a feeling of panic when you begin to make intentional efforts at being specific. Notwithstanding, it isn't something to worry about as it is a hundred percent normal.

Getting specific with your actions involved prioritizing, which, rather, unfortunately, adults with Attention-deficit/hyperactivity disorder find it very hard to do. This is because it forces you to say yes to some tasks, no matter how boring and uninteresting, such tasks might be, and then "no" to some other tasks – even if you feel like doing the "Nos" first. When you are confronted with a lot of tasks, saying just a temporary "no" may be very difficult for you, and sometimes even impossible. However, when you are specific with what you want to do, it won't be much of an issue anymore. And this is logical; the more specific you get, the more you find it easy to do the right things at the right time.

Write it down

No matter how intelligent and smart we may seem to be, we are still humans and are prone to forget things – we aren't computers, remember?

Thus, start writing what you are going to do for the day, as it helps a lot. Over time, you will discover that it is a great way to create a plan for yourself for the day. Instead of doing the regular (just whizzing those tasks in your head), write them down in places where you can see them.

Apart from the fact that it serves as a constant reminder throughout the day, it also helps in bettering your feeling of organization. Try it out today; write down the tasks that you are specific about doing today, and you will be surprised at how productive you can be.

Employ the two-minute rule.

As I have affirmed and re-affirmed over and over again in this book, one of the biggest barriers of productivity for persons with the Attention-deficit/hyperactivity disorder is procrastination. And, of course, this accounts for why this kind of individuals are characterized by missing deadlines, working under intense pressure, and so on. However, you can curb this up to an appreciable extent by employing the two-minute rule.

The two-minute rule, in the simplest of terms, is more like doing things always in the now. It programs your brain such that you begin to detest shifting tasks to the next day. Although, not that it wouldn't leave time for rest. For example, the two-minute rule will make you enter a new phone number into a database immediately you collect the digits, instead of keeping it for later which may ultimately cost you time as you may be caught in the web of looking for it or figuring out what a single number on a scrap of paper with no name goes to.

Pick a planner that works for you.

Persons with Attention-deficit/hyperactivity disorder tend to work more efficiently with structure. Factually, without structuration, you may be unable to achieve optimum productivity.

Structuring your activity includes having, planning, and maintaining a calendar. You should, however, know that when picking a planner, you must choose that which fits conveniently into your personal needs, and also one that you will eventually use.

Make time to plan.

Sometimes, productivity isn't only executing your tasks to the best of your capability. Yes, it is part, but it doesn't revolve around this in all entirety. Making out time every day to plan how your day will look like is also another simple yet crucial element that betters productivity, especially for adults who struggle with ADHD. Make out at least ten to twenty minutes to plan daily – setting aside this quota of time out of twenty-four hours won't kill you.

Use your calendar

In one of these strategies, I have mentioned that you should pick a planner (read like a calendar). In this regard, I advise that you make use of an online calendar, especially one that is connected to your phone, for example, the Google calendar.

You can make use of this calendar for appointments, meetings, conferences, and so on. This doesn't only make you have a clearer idea of what your week will look like, but also 1. It allows you to know how much work you've done. 2. It allows you to have easy access to your progress.

How to start a task

The first six strategies up there are basically to make you know what exactly you are going to work on and also when you have time to do it. Having known these, next, it is important that you develop enough trust in yourself that you will be able to start work on such tasks.

Whether you have the best intentions about such jobs or not, it is quite typical that you have a feeling of internal resistance towards starting such a task. It is normal; it's your nature – your kind of person. Albeit, it is imperative that you convince yourself of your good intentions, and tell yourself it's time to start.

For instance, when you say to yourself, "I am going to do B now," with intentional specificity, what you have just done is to override your brain's tendencies of restraining you from starting. Before you know what is happening, you will find yourself starting the task already.

How to keep going

Some adults with Attention-deficit/hyperactivity disorder may experience challenges to keep going on a task that they've started. In this case, distraction is playing a huge role. But then, it needs to be managed in other to keep going.

To keep going on a job, you need to shut both internal and external distractions. For internal distractions, set timers for yourself, give yourself benchmarks, and perhaps a promising reward for every task that you complete. This way, you will be able to maintain focus on such tasks.

For external distractions, you can switch your devices off, including your phones, too, except the device that you are making use of.

Don't Multi-Task!

As an adult struggling with ADHD, it is normal when you have an intense feeling or urge to multitask. Some people even take pride in being an excellent multi-tasker. But then, multi-tasking is all shades of wrong, especially when you are particular about how productive you are.

What you fail to know is that in the real sense, human brains can't actually multitask, rather the brain focuses only on one thing at a time. This infers that instead of multi-tasking as we think it to be, the brain actually rapidly shifts from one activity to another. These rapid shifts ultimately result in stress and fatigue, both of which reduce productivity.

What's being said in essence is that if you want to get things done better, do not multi-task.

New Email Habits

Checking your email inbox too often is a bad habit, as it also suffices as a means of multitasking. Whether you reply or not, checking your emails several times in just an hour reduces ample time that may be used for some other stuff. So, instead, you can resort to checking only twice or thrice per day.

Besides giving you more time and attention span, it also reduces stress. Overall, it allows you to do more daily.

Break things down

When having a large and seemingly overwhelming task at hand, it is advisable that you break such jobs down into simpler steps. However, when you are struggling with Attention-deficit/hyperactivity disorder, breaking the whole project down may turn out to be a great job itself. And this may either discourage you from doing it or ultimately lose both the motivation and time to get the job done.

So, instead, do not attempt to break the entire process down. Instead, simplify the job such that you know only the first step. Trust me, from there henceforth; other steps will surface automatically. Doing this will make such a project become lighter and clearer to do.

Declutter. But me super-selective when doing so.

Inarguably, clutters and lack of organization are great sources of a hindrance to productivity, as you may once in a while find yourself having to waste time looking for stuff that you need. Therefore, it is advisable that you allocate some of your time to decluttering. However, when doing so, ensure that you are super-selective and also paying attention to details too. This way, you will be sure of not taking important documents off your workspace or desk.

Understand the scope of a project.

Adults with ADHD have a high likelihood of being a perfectionist. However, rather unfortunately, perfectionism is yet another zapper of productivity that many people do not pay attention to. Albeit, when you know and understand the scope of a project, it allows you to know the extent of energy and effort you will invest in such a project. This way, you will save yourself from unnecessary actions that you may want to do to record success. You will be sure that you are doing what is being asked for, not more nor less.

Under-promise and over-deliver.

It is typical for persons with Attention-deficit/hyperactivity disorder to overpromise. And this may be because they underestimate how long they will take to complete a task. However, now is the time to begin to make intentional efforts at under-promising your clients, but in the end, surprise them with astonishing results. This also gets you more time to work on your projects.

Are you hungry?

By now, you already know that struggling with ADHD robs you of your focus. That is, you find it hard to focus. And, of course, lack of focus results in an inability to get things done. This explains why you need to eliminate anything that may want to deprive you of the utmost focus. One such distraction is hunger.

Ask yourself, are you hungry? If yes, it is advisable that you stop what you are doing and feed yourself.

Also, take note of what you eat. Certain foods, for example, protein, helps a great deal in bettering focus. You may want to include them in your diet too.

Enlist a productivity partner.

Instead of multitasking, you may want to enlist a productivity partner. Without gainsaying, having a support system (read as a partner) by your side helps tremendously with productivity. This caliber of persons can help you run errands, reply to emails, and all sorts of relatively simpler tasks. Partners in this regard may be friends, family, and so on. However, ensure that such a person is accountable.

Overall, Attention-deficit/hyperactivity disorder stops you from taking actions, prioritizing, and making decisions. Instead, on the other hand, it promotes procrastination, distraction, overthinking, multitasking, perfectionism, and the likes. Getting things done isn't as easy as they seem to be. Nonetheless, with the basic strategies discussed in this chapter, trust yourself to get back right on track, at least to an appreciable extent.

Albeit, as mentioned that these strategies are basic and may not be as quickly effective as you may require, the Pomodoro Technique has come to save the center stage in this regard. In the next chapter, I will be explaining everything that has to do with the Pomodoro Technique and its relationship with the Attention-deficit/hyperactivity disorder, including how it helps sufferers of ADHD to eliminate distractions, the resulting effects, and many more!

CHAPTER FOUR

POMODORO TECHNIQUES

In the simplest of terms, the Pomodoro Technique is a time management system; the encourages people to work *with* the time they have – rather than against it. Making use of this technique causes you to simplify your workday into a twenty-five-minute chunk, which is separated by a minimum of five-minute breaks. These breaks are what we refer to as Pomodoro. After about four to five breaks (read as Pomodoro), you can look into taking longer breaks, which may be as long as about fifteen to twenty minutes each.

Basically, the whole ideology about this Pomodoro of a thing is that the timer instills a feeling of urgency in persons that engage in it. So, as an adult with Attention-deficit/hyperactivity disorder whose normal thought is having endless time in the workday, the Pomodoro

Technique makes you want to get things done fast and timely without the presence of distractions, knowing fully well that you only have 25 minutes to make as much progress on a task as possible.

Besides, the forced breaks also help a great deal in curing that feeling of burn out that most of us tend to experience towards the end of the day. Normally, you may realize that you have to be in front of the computer the whole day yet without knowing. However, this timer serves as a reminder for you to stand up and get a breather. And this is actually logical. Getting breathers on the course of a job actually helps in preserving your sustainability on such a job. Overall, the Pomodoro Technique is was developed basically to make things much easier for you. This technique is quite simple, yet very effective!

Now, apart from helping you a great deal in getting things done, the Pomodoro Technique also helps adults with ADHD to learn how to work. This method helps you to master productivity skills in its entirety. We would be safe as well to say that the Pomodoro Technique offers an extensive range of advantages, with all, of course, boiling down to the elimination of distractions and bettering levels of productivity. In this regard, the Pomodoro Technique will help you to:

Planning tasks.

The Pomodoro Technique makes you create a to-do list that also suffices as a schedule. This to-do list is basically to ensure that you are as focused as possible on every one of your projects – you are expected to check off tasks that you have completed, and also to make extensive reviews of your next steps.

Starting and finishing tasks.

So, this is one of the main purposes of engaging in the Pomodoro Technique – to ensure that you do not start your "now" jobs immediately and also not to lose focus while on the job. And this is quite relatable – I mean, once the time begins, you are expected to set to work, and after a few timed sessions, trust me, you will be done! This way, you do not only get the job done but also timely.

Limiting distractions.

Once you start a session, your brain has been programmed to focus only on one thing. This way, distractions are greatly reduced, even if not completely eliminated. However, should distractions pop in your mind, knowing that you are in a timed session, then you jot them down only to attend to them much later.

Providing motivation.

The thing is, most likely; you will record success with making use of the Pomodoro Technique. This alone is enough source of motivation to keep making use of the technique to execute even larger and more difficult projects. Remember, as an adult struggling with ADHD, you need as much motivation as possible to get on a project and also keep the focus on that project.

Handling large tasks.

Recall that I mentioned in one of the previous chapters that you should inculcate the habit of breaking your projects into simpler tasks, such that you know the step to start with. Now, knowing that the Pomodoro Technique only allows you to work in sessions, 25 minutes (for beginners though), you are therefore compelled to break your tasks into smaller ones – as small as you are sure of completing within the set time for each session.

Avoid wasting time.

By engaging in the Pomodoro Technique, you may have just successfully eliminated the habit of wasting time when working on a job. How? The thing is that this technique positions your brain to believe that it has considerably lesser time to get a job done to its required perfection. So, this way, you go all way out, distractions and time-wasters eliminated until you get the job completed.

And also, even during your breaks, you are aware that these breaks are short and also timed. So, consequently, you may have just enough time to grab a snack or close your eyes and de-stress.

Setting objectives.

The Pomodoro Technique also causes you to create smaller goals at first, especially as a beginner, until you have eventually learned how much of work you can comfortably accomplish within 25 minutes. Over time, after a few more practices with the technique, trust me, your ability to set goals (also read as objectives) will improve.

Prioritizing tasks.

Breaking your tasks into smaller and manageable units helps you a great deal in prioritizing your to-do list; consequently, allowing you to learn which step to take first. With the Pomodoro Technique, getting what part to do first may never be an issue for you.

However, despite all of the several ways that the Pomodoro Technique helps an adult with ADHD to get their stuff done, I must say that this technique isn't a quick fix per se. In this regard, you should not count on mastering it on just a day or two. This infers that it is a gradual process, and it demands patience, time, persistence, energy, and commitment to actually hit the diamond with the technique. But trust me, it is worth it after all.

How the Pomodoro Technique Works

Dating back to the 80s when Francesco Cirillo invented the Pomodoro Technique, it has always been used as a personal system of getting more things done. Thus, bettering productivity level. And ever since Cirillo also released the whitepaper of how the Pomodoro Technique works, several successes have been recorded.

Albeit, the central idea behind the Pomodoro Technique is what is called "time boxing." As an adult struggling with Attention-deficit/hyperactivity disorder, more often than not, you may have been in a situation whereby you can't seem to start on a project. You must have, even more than once, taken a look at your to-do list and marked some tasks in your head that you think are too big to be completed, or you may never get done with. But then, you can't afford to fail or being desperate simply because you are having difficulties starting a task. And, in the same vein, you also can't afford to give up on working on your goals. Many times, what we result from doing is to continue to push these tasks down the list until we obviously can't do so any longer.

And then, this is where the Pomodoro Technique takes center stage. The main ideology behind the Pomodoro Technique is to beef up your attention for a small amount of time, and also cause you to recharge mentally after each work interval.

To engage in the Pomodoro Technique, all you need is a timer – also referred to as the Pomodoro. For starters, the Pomodoro Technique works in twenty-five minutes intervals. *The steps included are:*

1. Identify what the task at hand is.

What is the next task on your to-do list that needs to be done in the "now" time zone? Identify such a task and position yourself to start work on it.

2. Set your Pomodoro to 25 minutes.

Next, set your timer – the Pomodoro – to twenty-five minutes. Remember, you will be working with the timer; therefore, it is important that you are well-positioned to commence job on such a task. Get your head cleared, and also void of any form of distraction. You may switch your device(s) off too.

3. Work on the task until the Pomodoro is over.

Once you set the timer, begin work on the already identified task in step 1. Do not get your hands and mind off the job until the timer signals a stop. That is, until the end of twenty-five minutes.

4. Take a 5-minute break.

Thereafter, subject yourself to a compulsory five minutes of break. This period is where you are expected to mentally recharge yourself, grab, perhaps, a cup of ice or water, and maybe snacks, too, in preparation for the next session.

5. For every four Pomodoro, take a longer break (say 15-20 minutes).

You are expected to have repeated sessions until, of course, you record absolute success in such a task. But then, you may want to begin to take longer breaks, say about fifteen to twenty minutes of break, after every four Pomodoro sessions that you take. This way, you will be sure of having a completely recharged body system to go into the next bout of sessions.

This constraint set for oneself is one of the reasons that persons with Attention-deficit/hyperactivity disorder find this technique exclusively powerful! It makes you stay focused and ultimately do more.

Over time, I have realized that after completing a small part of a whole job, there's this natural momentum that envelops such a person, such that it keeps such a person going until he or she gets the job done completely. This must have happened to you before – it happens to everybody, anyway, not only persons with Attention-deficit/hyperactivity disorder. And this is exactly the kind of setting that persons with ADHD need, and will function with maximum effectiveness under. Hence, the need for the Pomodoro Technique.

The thing is, we see this scenario play out almost all the time as an individual that is battling with ADHD. This initial resistance holds us back from getting started on a job. However, once you get past this resistance, starting and completing such a task get exquisitely easier. To get past, you need to make use of the Pomodoro Technique!

Honestly, this is where the technique really shines. By subjecting yourself to time frames, you are giving yourself every possible reason to get started, which is synonymous with having just enough charge to fight the internal resistance stopping you from getting stuff done.

Do you always stop after 25 minutes?

From my wealth of experience, it is imperative that I mention the guidelines that I believe the Pomodoro Technique works by:

As a beginner, you may still have little bits of struggles with getting focused on the job during the timed sessions. In this regard, I advise that you stop work immediately the time rings.

If you are not a newbie at making use of the Pomodoro Technique and have recorded success several times, you may choose to continue with your work even after the timer goes off. This infers that you may use more than 25 minutes for each of your sessions, just that you need to be comfortable doing such and not merely forcing yourself.

Now, why I advise you as a newbie not to further with work after the Pomodoro (timer) goes off is to help you cultivate the habit of not only learning how to start but also how to stop. I have seen several persons get started with the Pomodoro Technique, get it right for the first few trials, but then do not learn how to stop once the timer goes off – the continue to work even after the timer runs out. This kind of person always ends up in the same ditch of procrastination, which turns out to be running in circles. I mean, what is the point of making use of the Pomodoro Technique yet without dropping the habit of procrastination!

Of course, I know you want to avoid being caught in similar webs too. That is why I have advised that you get used to using the technique first before anything else. And the interesting thing is that the more you can force yourself to start a task and keep your focus on such a task, the easier it always becomes to keep up with such a pace in the future, especially on things that you are scared of working on.

Basically, the timer herein is just a gimmick to ensure that you get started, and also to help you build the momentum needed for utmost productivity. Once you are used to making use of the timer and also going on breaks as much as they are needed, then you can proceed with the second guideline, as described earlier in this chapter. The scenario is, however, different per person. So, I also recommend that you engage in the technique under your belt before you consider going beyond the 25-minute benchmark.

Factually, several persons will increase their timers to roughly fifty to sixty minutes once they have mastered the technique. So, summarily, this is how it works; the starting 25 minutes forces you to eliminate traits (read as habits) of procrastination while extending the timer allows you more time to get focused on a job. Nonetheless, irrespective of the timer you are making use of, ensure that you are taking the necessary amounts of breaks.

How To Get Started With The Pomodoro Technique

Since a timer (Pomodoro) is the only crucial tool that you need to get started, you can, therefore, begin with a timer application on your phone. You may also make use of a countdown clock, or even a plain old egg timer. A manual timer may suffice for use too. In this regard, anyway, I have highlighted a few Pomodoro applications that you can make use of to serve as a timer. A few of these apps offer even more than what a simple timer offers anyway.

Marinara Timer

The Marinara Timer is a web application that you can keep open in a pinned tab. This application allows its users to choose their timer alerts such that they know when exactly to take a break, get back to work, and also reconfigure their work and break times to suit their pace, perhaps. It is free, easy to use, and appreciably flexible.

Tomighty (Win/Mac/Linux)

Tomighty is a cross-platform (Mac/Win/Linux) desktop Pomodoro Timer application. Tomighty allows its users to fire and forget, while on itself helps in following the traditional rules – the 25 minutes timer, and 5 minutes of break. Also, you may also customize your timing as it suits your preferences.

Eggcellent (Formerly called Pomodorable)

Eggcellent is an app that combines both timer and to-do. It also offers its users more visual information telling that you have either completed your tasks or what you have next. Eggcellent is compatible with macOS devices and integrated nicely with their apps too. With Eggcellent, you can even have an estimate of how much Pomodoro you will need to complete a job. You can also track your progress too.

Focus Timer (iOS)

Focus Timer is solely compatible with iPhone and iPad. With this Pomodoro App, you are allowed free access to customize your sessions and break periods too. It also allows its users to review their work history, and ultimately see how improved they have been with trying to keep their focus. You can also see how much time you have left for each of your sessions, and also a rating system to up your motivation game.

Basically, there are several Pomodoro applications in stores that can allow us to get started with the technique as adults struggling with Attention-deficit/hyperactivity disorder. We also have Google Calendar. Really, there are loads of timers available for you out there. You may also like to make use of the actual tomato timer like Cirillo did use. However, you should remember that your focus isn't really on the kind of timer you make use of but on the task that you need to do.

Chapter Five

Activities to do on

Pomodoro breaks

Okay, this is yet another important question that begs for an answer in this guide. Basically, you can be flexible with what you do during your Pomodoro breaks. I mean, it all boils down to one's preferences and what makes one relaxed. Some persons may just sit on the couch and have some water for relaxation during their breaks before hitting their next session. While on the other hand, some persons may opt for snacks, or exercises such as short walks around the neighborhood, stretching, and so on. Simply put – it depends on what you are comfortable with; there is no one-way guide to that.

Albeit, you may also want to try any of the options listed below during your break periods:

Some forms of simple exercises such as kettlebell swings, jumping jacks, pushups, and pull-ups.

Get busy with your choice of musical instruments, such as guitar, piano, and violin.

You may as well take a power nap.

- Read a book

- Juggle balls

- Consider stretching too.

Overall, the idea is to move away from your work desk during your break times. This way, you can be sure of having a mental break too from the work and workspace. In this regard, reading your emails or clearing your inbox during breaks aren't options that I will advise. I mean, this way, you are still engaging your brain!

When To Stop Pomodoro In A Day

Without fantasizing or gainsaying, as the case may be, there is actually no such thing as an eight-hour workday.

See things this way; within the acclaimed eight hours of work, there are moments that you will go for lunch, prayers, water cooler talks, meetings, checking of emails, and so on. Subtracting all the minutes used for these activities, you may be left with maybe just 4-5 hours. So, you too, you see that the 8-hour workday may just be a myth. But then, everybody has different jobs, which translates to having different tasks to overcome, and also different commitments. In this regard, we may be safe to agree that there isn't really any fast rule for how many Pomodoro sessions you need to do per day.

Truth be told, it all boils down to your personal capabilities. For some persons with ADHD, they can go up to four Pomodoro in a day, which is about two hours of exclusive and total focus on their job, which, of course, is quite promising too. While for some, they may go up to 6 or 7. As I have mentioned, it all depends on how long you can sustain yourself. But then, you do not need to get hard on yourself, especially when you are just starting out with the Pomodoro Technique. Remember, you can't achieve excellent results immediately, it is a gradual process.

But then, the minimum I recommend per-say is 2 Pomodoro sessions. This translates to about an hour of total concentration. If you can't do this, then you may be having even greater problems to deal with.

Nonetheless, the Pomodoro Technique is a very excellent way of beating procrastination at the start of the day. It is no longer news that you are characterized by procrastination (which may not be the same as laziness), so getting out of the bed may seem like a great task for you to overcome. But then, you may rejoice as the Pomodoro Technique is here to the rescue!

For some adults with the Attention-deficit/hyperactivity disorder, they only make use of the Pomodoro Technique to get started with the day after which they discard its use for the day till the next. I'm mentioning all these to affirm that you can make use of this technique at your own liking and preferences and comfortability level because how you make use of it isn't was matters per se; rather, what matters is that you are getting your works done.

Set a 25-minute timer for yourself now for your next task, after which you can then take a break. Ensure that you are committed to only focus on just one task and nothing else. As a starter, do not go past the 25-minute benchmark. Once it goes off, take a walk-off your desk for 5 minutes of break. Having done this, congratulations as you have just completed your first Pomodoro! – try it out today!

Having said this, I want you to start seeing the Pomodoro Technique as a tool that you can make use of at a time that you're convenient with. Make use of these suitable moments, especially if you know that you may procrastinate during these times.

To some certain extent, you can only read as much as possible about the Pomodoro Technique and how it suffices as a savior for adults struggling with Attention-deficit/hyperactivity disorder. However, you just have to try it our personally to see for yourself if it works for you, or otherwise. Well, I am more than confident that the former will be the case for you. With time as well, you will find yourself getting continuously productive, even more than you have been in the past, yet without experiencing burnouts.

Who the Pomodoro Technique works best for?

The Pomodoro Technique basically work best for adults who are struggling with Attention-deficit/hyperactivity disorder and are as the same time designers, developers, or any other person who may be directly or indirectly concerned with packing creative works. In essence, I am referring to individuals who are connected to producing things to be reviewed by others. This translates that everyone, ranging from authors to software engineers, and so on who are struggling with ADHD can all enjoy the benefits that Pomodoro Technique has to offer.

Similarly, Pomodoro is useful for individuals who do not have as rigid goals or packages of work as expected or as much as possible. Should you also have a long queue of tasks that demands to be completed, then you may also enjoy the timed sessions too.

As an adults with Attention-deficit/hyperactivity disorder who's also a system engineer, the timed sessions allow you to start working through your system as soon as the timer starts and compels that you stop once it goes off, in other to stake the compulsory breaks (revert to earlier sections of this chapter for a better knowledge of things to do during breaks). And the same thing scheme also applies to others too. Basically, Pomodoro Technique is remarkably adaptable and compatible to as much kinds of work as possible – I haven't taking note of any form of considerable restrictions so far.

What if I still get distracted?

Okay, so, you have comfortably and assuredly blocked all forms of distractions, including your websites, gaming consoles, and so on, and consequently set your timer. But then, there are still certain extents of likelihood that someone, maybe your coworker, family, and so on, will pass by with a question or drop by for an urgent response from time to time. In this regard, what then do you do, as it seems to be a scenario that is past your reasonable capabilities?

First, it is important that you know and understand that the Pomodoro Technique is a unit of work that can't actually be separated from the whole. This means that if you experience any form of distraction(s) during any of your pomodoro sessions, it is either you have to end such session at that point and resort to starting a new one later, or you will have to postpone such a distraction to some much better time, perhaps when you are done with the session. In essence, you cannot possibly pause a Pomodoro session to attend to a distraction. You should know that there is absolutely nothing like "partial Pomodoro." Why? Well, the thing is, when distracted under normal circumstances, it takes approximately 23 minutes to successfully refocus, which in itself is almost the time for a complete Pomodoro session.

But then, certainly, there is way by which you can control such kinds of interruptions (read as distractions) – interpretation. This translates that by proper interpretation of such distractions, an adult with Attention-deficit/hyperactivity disorder can perfectly take control and address them in the best of ways such that he or she still remains productive. After all, that distraction can wait for about 25 minutes of even less – until you are done with your session.

What the Pomodoro Technique teaches adults essentially are effective and efficient ways of managing all forms of distraction, not just anyhow, but in ways that it boosts the overall productivity of such an adult and also allow them to take total control of their time. In this regard, the founder of the Pomodoro Technique, Cirillo, has explained that the best way to deal with distractions aforehand and to also manage priorities as someone with Attention-deficit/hyperactivity disorder is to employ the "inform, negotiate and call back" strategy. What this strategy teaches is quite simple:

Inform: this implies that you inform your source of distraction that you are busy with a task as the moment and may not be able to attend to him or her.

Negotiate: Negotiating expects you to agree with your source of distraction on the exact time you will get back to them.

Schedule: remember that as a result of the Attention-deficit/hyperactivity disorder you are struggling with, you tend to forgets things quite easily. In this regard, it is imperative that you schedule such a follow-up immediately.

Call back: when you are done with your Pomodoro session, ensure that you call back as and when you have promised.

When you often have issues with unplanned distractions during Pomodoro Sessions, I advise that you religiously follow the strategy explained above.

CONCLUSION

Attention-deficit/hyperactivity disorder (ADHD) isn't a death sentence; neither is understanding the disorder in its entirety, and what works in its regard isn't and shouldn't be seen as rocket science. Well, we may be safe to say that ADHD is also a way of life.

As much as you may find it quite difficult and challenging to get things done timely and efficient, you should know that there are a few available ways of getting your stuff done. ADHD shouldn't be an obstacle, after all!

In this guide, I have taken out time to comprehensively capture the entire scope of Attention-deficit/hyperactivity disorder, and of course, how to get stuff done when you are struggling with the disorder, including the Pomodoro Technique.

As an adult struggling with ADHD, you may be confronted with several issues, which may result in many unfavorable consequences, especially when not managed properly. In this regard, I strongly recommend that you religiously put the information shared in this guide to using, most notably, the Pomodoro Technique. With this, trust me, you are good to go!

I understand the extent of frustration that may come alongside failing to beat deadlines, no matter how much you try. Nonetheless, trust this guide to put you in the right path of managing your Attention-deficit/hyperactivity disorder.

Love & Light from me to you. Cheers!